How Do Wind and Water Change Earth?

Change Earth?

Natalie Hyde

 Crabtree Publishing Company

www.crabtreebooks.com

Author
Natalie Hyde

Publishing plan research and development
Reagan Miller

Editor
Crystal Sikkens

Proofreader and indexer
Wendy Scavuzzo

Design
Samara Parent

Photo research
Tammy McGarr

Prepress technician
Tammy McGarr

Print and production coordinator
Margaret Amy Salter

Photographs
iStock: TOC © Linda Kloosterhof
Thinkstock: p6 Fuse; p 20 (sand); p22 keithfrith

All other images from Shutterstock

Library and Archives Canada Cataloguing in Publication

Hyde, Natalie, 1963-, author
   How do wind and water change Earth? / Natalie Hyde.

(Earth's processes close-up)
Includes index.
Issued in print and electronic formats.
ISBN 978-0-7787-1727-0 (bound).--ISBN 978-0-7787-1773-7 (paperback).--
ISBN 978-1-4271-1610-9 (pdf).--ISBN 978-1-4271-1606-2 (html)

      1. Erosion--Juvenile literature. 2. Weathering--Juvenile literature.
I. Title.

QE571.H94 2015   j551.3'02   C2015-903933-9
                                       C2015-903934-7

Library of Congress Cataloging-in-Publication Data

Hyde, Natalie, 1963-
   How do wind and water change Earth? / Natalie Hyde.
      pages cm. -- (Earth's processes close-up)
   ISBN 978-0-7787-1727-0 (reinforced library binding) --
   ISBN 978-0-7787-1773-7 (pbk.) --
   ISBN 978-1-4271-1610-9 (electronic pdf) --
   ISBN 978-1-4271-1606-2 (electronic html)
   1. Winds--Juvenile literature. 2. Water--Juvenile literature. 3. Earth
(Planet)--Surface--Juvenile literature. I. Title.
   QC931.4.H84 2016
   551.3'5--dc23
                           2015024023

Crabtree Publishing Company

Printed in Canada/112022/CPC20221107

www.crabtreebooks.com   1-800-387-7650

Published in Canada
Crabtree Publishing
616 Welland Ave.
St. Catharines, Ontario
L2M 5V6

Published in the United States
Crabtree Publishing
PMB 59051
350 Fifth Avenue, 59th Floor
New York, New York 10118

Published in the United Kingdom
Crabtree Publishing
Maritime House
Basin Road North, Hove
BN41 1WR

Published in Australia
Crabtree Publishing
3 Charles Street
Coburg North
VIC 3058

Contents

Our changing Earth

Earth is always on the move. Some forces are building up new **landforms**. Other forces are wearing them down. Wind, water, and ice can break large landforms into small pieces. This process is called weathering. Some changes happen quickly. Other changes happen slowly. Weathering is a slow process.

Weathering creates interesting rock shapes.

Bit by bit

Slow changes are hard to see. Mountains might take thousands of years to wear away. Only a few small rocks might break off each year. A river can change its **course** over time. This would be hard to notice, since it might only move 1 inch (2.5 cm) every few years.

Water can freeze in the cracks of huge rocks. Over time, ice can break the rocks apart into small pieces.

Wind erosion

Air that moves is called wind. Wind can be gentle like a breeze. It can also be very strong in a storm. The Sun warms the air. Warm air is lighter than cold air. Warm air rises and cold air rushes in to replace it. This is what makes wind blow.

You can feel the wind blowing on your face.

Moving Earth

Wind can pick up and move tiny bits of rock and soil. Sometimes it can carry these pieces long distances before dropping them. Moving material from one place to another is called erosion.

*Sand is made up of tiny pieces of rock. Sometimes wind moves sand into large piles. The piles of sand are known as **sand dunes**.*

Wind weathering

The tiny bits of sand and rock carried by the wind can also blow against landforms. This can cause other pieces of rock to break off. When this happens, it is known as wind weathering. The blowing pieces of rock wear away at the landform like **sandpaper**.

Some rocks can be weathered until they are smooth and flat.

Sandstorms happen when strong winds carry large amounts of sand in the air.

Shaped by the wind

The wind cannot lift bits of sand and rock very high. So, they weather huge rocks near the ground. This can create strangely shaped rocks. The rocks become narrow at the bottom, but stay wide at the top.

Would you see more landforms weathered by wind in a cold, frozen desert or in a hot, sandy desert? Why?

Weathered rocks look a lot like mushrooms.

Water

Water covers almost three-quarters of Earth. It flows through rivers and streams, and falls to the ground as rain or snow. As it moves, it changes Earth's surface.

Moving water wears away the rocks and soil it flows over. It also picks up and carries bits of soil, sand, and rocks, and drops them in new places.

*Water moves more **earth** than any other process.*

Fast water

The faster the water moves, the more material it carves out. Streams are small bodies of moving water. They wear away **channels** over many years. Floods can make big changes to Earth's surface quickly. Floodwaters can move huge rocks long distances. They can carve out new channels in a few hours.

Water flowing at only 4 miles per hour (6 kph) is very powerful. It can move huge rocks that are 5 feet (1.5 m) across!

Oceans and tides

An ocean is a huge body of salt water. Oceans are always moving. The water level on the shore rises and falls. This is called the tide. As the tide goes in and out, it can bring sand and rocks with it. Tides move material slowly. Over time though, rocks and sand can travel a long distance.

When the tide goes out, a little water gets trapped in holes between the rocks. These are called tide pools.

Wave power

Wind blowing over the surface of the water creates waves. Ocean waves pound rocks on the shore. The pounding slowly breaks them down into tiny grains of sand. The sand builds up to form beaches.

Is it possible for sand dunes to be found at the beach? Why or why not?

Beach sand can be many different colors. The color depends on what kinds of rocks and minerals were weathered to make it.

13

Rivers and streams

A river or stream is **fresh water** that flows across Earth's surface. Streams often empty into rivers, and rivers empty into lakes or oceans. As they flow, rivers and streams carve out channels or **canyons**. They remove soil and sand and can carry it long distances.

The Colorado River has been carving out the Grand Canyon for millions of years.

14

Sandbars

Rivers and streams drop the material they carry wherever the water slows down. This creates new landforms. A pile of sand in a river or along a shore is called a sandbar. Sandbars can move if the flow of the water changes.

A river can leave soil where it meets a lake or ocean. This builds up in a triangle-shaped area called a delta.

Water from the sky

Water can fall from clouds as rain, hail, or snow. Every time water hits the surface, it can cause changes. Raindrops gather chemicals from the air. These chemicals eat away at Earth's surface after it rains. Rain can also seep into cracks in rocks. When the rain freezes, it changes to ice and **expands**. This can cause the rock to break into pieces.

Over a long period of time, raindrops can carve out holes in solid rock.

Hail is frozen balls of water. It can damage plants when it hits Earth's surface.

Sliding away

When rain hits soil or sand, it can turn them into mud. Muddy soil can begin to move and slide. The more rain that falls, the looser the soil becomes. An entire side of a mountain can slide away if the soil gets too wet. This is called a landslide.

What changes can rain cause to Earth's surface?

Frozen water

In areas with cold temperatures, water freezes into a solid. Snow, hail, and ice are all types of frozen water. Snow does not melt at the top of the highest mountains. Layers of snow build up. They become so heavy, they press the bottom layers into ice. The ice begins to slowly slide down the mountain like a river.

A frozen river of ice is called a glacier.

Ice carving

Glaciers are very heavy. They carve out valleys as they move. Everything in their path is pushed ahead of them. Piles of soil and rock are moved by the glacier. They create new landforms when the glacier melts.

It takes millions of years for a glacier to carve a valley.

River of ice activity

Glaciers have a big effect on landforms. Their weight and movement cause changes to the ground under them. This activity will show you some of the ways glaciers change the surface of Earth.

You will need:

ice cube

paper towels

modeling clay

shallow box or tray

sand

Steps

1. Flatten a small ball of clay onto the tray.
2. Move the ice cube back and forth over the clay several times. Look for changes in the surface of the clay.
3. Now place some sand on top of the clay. Put the ice cube on top of the sand and leave it for one minute.
4. Pick up the ice cube and look at the side that was touching the sand. What do you see?
5. Place the sandy ice cube back on the clay. Press it down, and move it back and forth several times.
6. Remove the ice cube. Use a paper towel to gently brush the sand off the clay.

Asking questions

- What changes did you notice on the surface of the clay after you rubbed the sandy ice cube on it?
- What do you think would happen if the sand was replaced with bigger rocks?
- How does this activity teach us how glaciers change the surface of Earth?

Studying changes

Scientists are trying to learn more about erosion and weathering. Some experts are looking at how water moves sand and soil along shorelines. This will help them plan ahead for changes. They want to protect homes for birds and other animals. They also want to avoid dangers for ships, such as moving sandbars.

Waves from strong storms can wash away beach sand.

Learning more

Books

Cracking Up: A Story About Erosion by Jacqui Bailey, Picture Window Books, 2006.

Sand on the Move: The Story of Sand Dunes by Roy Gallant, Franklin Watts, 1998.

What is wind? by Robin Johnson, Crabtree Publishers, 2012.

Websites

Learn about weathering and erosion at Geology For Kids: **www.kidsgeo.com/geology-for-kids/0060-weathering.php**

Follow student researcher Liz Jackson in this great video about weathering and erosion: **http://schoolmediainteractive.com/view/object/clip/6EF46CAA2D38E0EABB11A57BAFFB1753**

A great slideshow showing images of erosion and weathering: **www.slideshare.net/MMoiraWhitehouse/weathering-erosion-and-depositioneasier**

Words to know

canyons (KAN-yuh nz) noun Deep valleys with steep sides

channels (CHAN-ls) noun Straight passages

course (kohrs) noun The path a river takes

earth (urth) noun Soil and dirt

expands (ik-SPANDS) verb Gets larger

fresh water (fresh WOT-er) noun Water that does not have salt in it

landforms (LAND-fawrms) noun Features on Earth's surface

sand dunes (sand doons) noun Mounds or ridges of sand built by the wind

sandpaper (SAND-pey-per) noun Paper with sand glued to it and used to smooth wood

> A noun is a person, place, or thing. A verb is an action word that tells you what someone or something does.

Index

24

Earth's Processes Close-Up

Earth's Landforms
and Bodies of Water

Earthquakes, Eruptions, and
Other Events that Change Earth

How Do Wind and Water
Change Earth?

Protecting Earth's Surface

Guided Reading: L

CRABTREE
PUBLISHING COMPANY
WWW.CRABTREEBOOKS.COM

Teacher's Guide

www.crabtreebooks.com/
resources/teachers-guides

ISBN 978-0-7787-1773-7

9 780778 717737

90000 >

Engineering
in our
Everyday
Lives

Reagan Miller